SPIRITUAL COMPLEMENT

SPIRITUAL COMPLEMENT
The Heart of Christianity

Book 2
in the Series
"The Heart of Christianity"

A Complementary Work
to—
SPIRITUAL SUBSTANCE

Inspiration, instruction, and practical direction for The Spiritual Life

---

Orison de Corde

Copyright © 2019 by **Orison de Corde**
All rights reserved.

Kindle Direct Publishing

"Orison de Corde"
is the author's nom de plume.

Includes excerpts, edited and adapted, from the following works—
  Grou, John Nicholas. *Manual for Interior Souls*. London: S. Anselms Society, Copyright © 1890.
  Lallemant, Louis. *The Spiritual Doctrine of Father Louis Lallemant*. London: Burns & Lambert, Copyright © 1855.
  Grou, John Nicholas. *Spiritual Maxims*. London: J. T. Hayes, Copyright © 1874.

———

Spiritual Complement/Orison de Corde. – 1st ed.
ISBN-13: 978-1086015959

Through the Immaculate Heart of Mary

CONTENTS

Books of the Bible Abbreviations

SPIRITUAL COMPLEMENTS

   1. Commentary on *"The Way of Christ"* 3

   2. The Sacred Heart of Jesus 9

   3. Supernatural Virtues and the
       Gifts of the Holy Spirit 13

   4. Ora et Labora 17

   5. Spiritual Works of Mercy 21

PRAYERFUL POETRY & PROVERBS

   Humility & Obedience
   Add up to Love (Poem 1) 25

   The Joy of Suffering (Poem 2) 28

   Confirmation (Poem 3) 30

   PROVERBS 33

THE SPIRITUAL LIFE: SOME MORE NOTES

   The Spiritual Life: Some More Notes 37

SPIRITUAL SELECTIONS

   Fundamental Truths of the Interior Life
   (Manual for Interior Souls) 47

   On The Means of Attaining Virtue
   (Manual for Interior Souls) 59

   On the Violence We Must Use
   To Die to Ourselves
   (Manual for Interior Souls) 73

On the Annihilation of Self
(Manual for Interior Souls) 83

On the Human Heart
(Manual for Interior Souls) 87

On the Guidance of the Holy Spirit
(The Spiritual Doctrine) 93

Devotion to Our Lord
(Spiritual Maxims) 103

*Quotations from the Holy Bible
throughout this book
are a literal synthesis or blending
of several translations.
They are not to be interpreted or used as
official translations
of the Sacred Scriptures.*

Books of the Bible
Abbreviations

OLD TESTAMENT
(No Abbreviations)

NEW TESTAMENT

Matt	Matthew	1 Tim	1 Timothy
Mark	Mark	2 Tim	2 Timothy
Luke	Luke	Titus	Titus
John	John	Philem	Philemon
Acts	Acts	Heb	Hebrews
Rom	Romans	James	James
1 Cor	1 Corinthians	1 Peter	1 Peter
2 Cor	2 Corinthians	2 Peter	2 Peter
Gal	Galatians	1 John	1 John
Eph	Ephesians	2 John	2 John
Phil	Philippians	3 John	3 John
Col	Colossians	Jude	Jude
1 Thes	1 Thessalonians	Rev	Revelation
2 Thes	2 Thessalonians		

SPIRITUAL COMPLEMENTS

Chapter 1

Commentary on *"The Way of Christ"*

"Make love your aim."
(1 Cor. 14:1)

In our walk with the Lord Jesus Christ we are working toward a definite goal: the union of our will with God's will. Why do we focus on offering up our will instead of our mind or body, for example? The will is the master-faculty insofar as it commands or directs all the other faculties or powers of our soul and body which are subject to it, that is, all that is voluntary. Moreover, the will is represented by the heart, and in Sacred Scripture the word "heart," when used figuratively, indicates the source and center of our life, strength and desires, including our mind, soul and spirit.

For example, "Trust in the Lord with all your heart, and lean not on your own understanding."—Proverbs 3:5 or "Create in me a pure heart, O God, and renew within me a right spirit."—Psalms 51:10 or "You will seek Me and find Me when you seek Me with all your heart." (Jeremiah 29:13) Therefore, by offering up our will and asking for God's will in return, we are giving God all that we have, all that we are, to do with as He pleases. We are loving God and being united to Him because the will's activity is to love, and love unites the lover with the beloved. Thus we attain union with God and come to love Him above all things by giving Him our will—our heart, our love. However, in order for us to be able to give up our will to God we must deal with sin and its countless effects.

Sin binds our will in a tight knot and hinders us from freely loving God and our neighbor. In being inherently selfish, sin can only love itself. Thus self-love, an effect of pride, is our greatest enemy. We go right to the source of the trouble when we begin to deal with sin through repentance, penance, and reparation. By God's grace we can conquer the sin within and practice the opposite virtues, thereby freeing our will from the chains of self-love and return our love back to God. By dealing with pride and anger through the humility and meekness of Christ, we strike at the source of all our evils. So here we see the sound basis for practicing The Four Step Prayer in *The Way of Christ* as well as the nightly examination of conscience.

Although all seven of the capital sins (vices) reside inside of us to some degree or another until we are purified and brought to perfection, it is profitable to work hardest on our most predominant fault because all of the sins weaken and die together, and, consequently, we will make great gains in all areas of our spiritual life and growth in virtue by removing the main obstacle, by the grace of God. Yet, while this is true, it remains necessary to die to our pride, especially, because it is the root cause of all sin and holds the whole structure of the "old man" together. As humility is the spiritual disposition, attitude and intention behind all true love and virtue, all grace and glory, so pride is the perverse power, the spiritual disorder, behind all self-centeredness and sin, all evil and vainglory.

The action of offering our will to God in

The Four Step Prayer includes the action of letting go of our own false concepts or ideas about who we are or should be, about what we need or have coming, about the nature of true love, and so forth. All of our concepts or ideas not in conformity with the Gospel of Jesus Christ are obstacles to union with God because God is "the Spirit of truth" and "God is love"—infinite, uncreated and eternal. (John 16:13)(1 John 4:16) "Eye has not seen, ear has not heard, nor has the heart of man conceived, what God has prepared for those who love Him." (1 Cor. 2:9) As we deny ourselves, pick up our cross daily, and follow Jesus, these false concepts or ideas, these untrue imaginings, false presuppositions or erroneous assumptions, begin to burst by the enlightenments of the Holy Spirit, and we are left with concepts or ideas more in line with the truth. Eventually, through the gift of infused contemplation and the supernatural light of divine illumination our mind will be purified, put in order, and brought to rest in "the peace of God, which surpasses all understanding." (Phil. 4:7) We will be freed from the need to think or meditate continually, especially in our relationship with God, now that our heart and soul and mind have been united to God more fully in the Living Flame of Love. We will know the Truth, and the Truth will set us free. (John 8:32)

The ideas or concepts that we have which do correspond with reality to some degree have a kernel of truth in them which will remain after the imaginary rind has been burned away—absorbed and removed—by the Flame of Love in divine contemplation. Even so, the candle light of human reason will be superseded by the warm bright light of the "Sun" with its powerful rays of divine wisdom and supernatural love. "I am that 'Sun,' God eternal, from which proceed the Son and the Holy Spirit,... and we are one and the same 'Sun.'" (*The Dialogue of St. Catherine of Siena*) Increasingly, we will no longer be ruled by our imagination and passions, or even by human reason enlightened by faith (as good as that is for spiritual beginners), but by the gentle guidance and gifts of the Holy Spirit and the circumstances of Divine Providence.

In our spiritual journey, the devil (our enemy) tries to block the way to union with God by interfering. As we grow closer to God in the spiritual life, we will become better at recognizing the approach or presence of the evil one—"Watch and pray, that you may not enter into temptation." (Matt. 26:41) Reject the temptation or distraction, the disquieting thought or desire that disturbs your peace, through Jesus Christ our Lord, and through the Immaculate Heart of Mary, praying immediately in whatever way works best for you. Then, continue with the duty or action of the present moment, according to God's will.

Chapter 2

The Sacred Heart of Jesus

You have granted me the priceless gift
of Your familiar friendship,
giving me,
to my indescribable delight,
the noblest treasure
of the divinity,
Your divine heart,
exchanging it with mine,
as a sign of our mutual familiarity,
bestowing it freely.
—St. Gertrude the Great

Most Sacred Heart of Jesus, I give my heart to You! You are the heart of every Christian home, of every Christian family, of every human heart in love with You. You are the heart of every Catholic Church, of every Catholic Mass, of every Holy Eucharist. You are the heart of everything, Most Sacred Heart of Jesus. We adore You in the most Holy Eucharist. We come to You in the deepest recesses of our soul. Make us whole. Fill us full. We implore Your Sacred Heart for everything we need, especially for our need of love. O Most Sacred Heart of Jesus, fill my heart with love for You!

Your love is strong and stable. Your love is pure and unconditional, no strings attached, and humble. Your love is sincere and honest, good as gold coming from the Fire of Charity. Your love is true and real, free of all adultery, dishonesty and deceit. Your love is never shallow or hollow, empty or vain, but full of all goodness, truth, and beauty.

Here we find, in Your Most Sacred Heart, humility and meekness—the remedy for all self-pity, anger, pride and hardheartedness. "Learn of me, for I am meek and humble of heart." (Matt. 11:29)

Here we find all purity, in mind and heart, soul and body—the remedy for self-centered self-love and the darkness and death of lust. "Blessed are the pure of heart, for they shall see God." (Matt. 5:8)

Here we find all true love—the remedy for a broken or lonely heart. "Was not our heart burning within us *(from the Fire of Charity)*, while He spoke to us on the way." (Luke 24:32)

Here we find, in Your Most Sacred Heart, Lord Jesus, true peace of heart—for "You have made us for Yourself, O Lord, and our heart is restless until it rests in You." (St. Augustine, *The Confessions)*

Chapter 3

Supernatural Virtues and the Gifts of the Holy Spirit

*We who as yet do not partake so abundantly
of the gifts of the Holy Spirit must labor and toil
in the practice of virtue.
We are like those who make way
by dint of rowing against wind and tide;
a day will come, if it please God, when,
having received (more abundantly) the gifts
of the Holy Spirit, we shall speed full-sail
before the wind; for it is the Holy Spirit
who by his gifts disposes the soul to yield itself
easily to his divine inspirations.*
—*Father Louis Lallemant*

Supernatural union with God requires supernatural grace to attain. We pray for and practice the virtues to grow in grace and virtue for "whoever has his mind set on virtue shall be greatly endowed with virtues from above." (St. Bede the Venerable) We grow in union with God by loving Him above all things and our neighbor as ourself. Therefore, we grow in union with God by practicing the virtues—including our prayer life—according to His wisdom and will, because "Virtue is nothing but well-directed love." (St. Augustine) We love God by practicing virtue and we practice virtue by the love of God. Sometimes it is simply the virtue of accepting, with humility and true love, the cross of the present moment, letting go of our own will and expectations. Our Lady of Lourdes famously said to St. Bernadette, "I do not promise you happiness in this life, but in the next." We can expect the cross to be with us, some days more than others, until the life to come, but we can also expect God to never leave us and to draw us closer to Himself, through Christ our Lord. To suffer is not a sin, but the opportunity to grow in grace and virtue, in union with God, by accepting the cross with Christ Crucified and Risen. At the same time, we actively practice the virtues in cooperation with the grace of God, "Deny yourself, pick up your cross daily, and follow me"—body and soul—and become more humble and holy, more innocent and pure, more loving and forgiving, more strong and mature—humanly and spiritually. (Luke 9:23) Consequently, "Virtue demands courage, constant effort, and, above all, help from on high." (St. John Vianney)

Furthermore, we need the supernatural virtues and gifts of the Holy Spirit to free us from the evil one. Consider St. Paul's exhortation, "Put on the whole armor of God, that you may be able to stand against the deceits of the devil. For our wrestling is not against flesh and blood, but against principalities and powers, against the rulers of this world's darkness, against the evil spirits in the high places." (Eph. 6:11-13) In particular, we need the supernatural virtues of faith, hope, and charity, and the supernatural gifts of the Holy Spirit—divine wisdom, understanding, knowledge, counsel, fortitude, loving devotion, and the fear of the Lord. All of these virtues and gifts of the Holy Spirit may be experienced as a single supernatural spiritual instinct, containing both insight and impulse (for or against something), that by following frees us from the evil one, sin and temptation, or even just distraction, and—if it is truly from God—always leads us into greater peace and the presence of God, because we are doing His will.

Chapter 4

Ora et Labora

*The first end I propose in our daily work is
to do the Will of God;
secondly, to do it in the manner He wills it;
and thirdly, to do it because it is His Will.*
—St. Elizabeth Ann Seton

The Holy Spirit blows where He will like the wind. So is everyone born-again. (John 3:8) We also know that the Holy Spirit is given to all who obey God. (Acts 5:32) God always does His part by blowing our soul in the right direction with correction and love, opening and closing doors, inspiring good ideas and desires, or warning us that something is not right, out of order, spiritually suffocating or misleading us away from God's will. But do we do our part by obeying His Word and go with the flow of humility and true love, avoiding unnecessary entanglements, practicing prayer and virtue and not give in to spiritual laziness or acedia, anger or self-pity, lustful thoughts or desires, prideful self-importance, restless greed or gnawing covetousness?

Jesus is there, always drawing us into a deeper relationship with God, calling us to follow Him. We respond to this loving and peaceful invitation with our cooperation—we "pray and work" *("ora et labora")*—according to God's will. (Benedictine Motto)

In prayer, we experience God's presence and come to know Him in a personal way. We pray for what we need, and we thank God for everything. In work, we love God in action by fulfilling our daily duties in order to please Him and out of love for others. Mary and Martha (prayer and work) must be blended and balanced in such a way as to lift our mind and heart to God during the day. Like the two wings of a dove, we pray during the day as we work for God and others and are lifted up above our lower nature into the air of divine love. We need both wings of the dove (prayer and work) to be successful. If either one is missing, we will not rise above the world but will crawl on the ground like inchworms. Fly into the sky with the help of the Holy Spirit by praying during the day in your own way as you do God's will in your work. God will not do everything (that is the lie of Quietism) because He respects our free will and human reason and expects us to use them. We cannot do everything (that is the heresy of Pelagianism) because union with God is our goal and only He can lift us up to union with Him. Teamwork is what we need—God and us working together for the human and spiritual betterment of ourselves and others—all for the honor and glory of God and the salvation of souls. We can always win the battle against sin, practice prayer and virtue, and love God and our neighbor—with God on our side (and we on His).

Chapter 5

Spiritual Works of Mercy

All the world together
is not worth
one soul.
—St. Augustine

The Seven "Spiritual Works of Mercy" are—

(1) <u>To convert</u> the sinner, by the grace of God, from seeking to do their own will to seeking to do the will of God, through Jesus Christ our Lord.

(2) <u>To instruct or enlighten</u> the unaware of spiritual truths or realities in a way that leads them closer to God.

(3) <u>To counsel</u> the doubtful in the ways of God and the spiritual life that they might fulfill His will more wholeheartedly and more fully.

(4) <u>To spiritually console</u> in spirit the sorrowful or suffering by way of prayer and penance, spiritual word or religious deed.

(5) <u>To patiently accept crosses</u> that come from others, including persecution or injustice, until God removes them from us or leads us to freedom.

(6) <u>To forgive</u>, by the grace of God, those who have hurt us.

(7) <u>To pray</u> for the living, especially, for their conversion, sanctification and salvation. Or, <u>to pray</u> for those who have died and are in Purgatory being purified, that they may enter Heaven as soon as possible by God's mercy.

PRAYERFUL POETRY
&
PROVERBS

Humility & Obedience Add up to Love
Poem 1

Most Holy Trinity,
through Mary, our Mother,
fill Thy Castle, Holy Church,
with Thy blessings throughout the earth.

Holy Angels protect and guide us,
to the Heavenly Fountain's abode.

On the road of salvation lead us,
for with Christ we journey forth.

Out of sin and darkness wailing,
into light and life unfailing.

Lead Thy poor and wretched servants,
unto truth, once again.
For with time and with Thy grace,

we can find the Key of Life.

Jesus Christ, the Key of Life,
will lead us to the Cross divine.

Holy Cross, in Thy arms,
we find rest from all that harms.

Holy Cross, we come to Thee,
help us in our misery.

For on that Cross we find our home,
but not without the pain of death.

Dying to sin and rising again,
this is the truth of the cross we share,
this is the cost of the cross we bear.

Jesus Christ will never leave us,
only we must bear the pain.

Simple love in obedience sowing,
for eternal life begun.

Only Jesus can free our souls
from sin and death and evil
for all time.
Only Jesus can show us meekness,
and the gift of truth in humility.

Humility and obedience add up to Love.
Love for the Father, our God above.
Love for the Son, the Only Begotten One.
Love for His Mother, Mary so pure.
Love for the Spirit of God residing
in holy souls in truth abiding.
Love for the saints and angels of God.
Love for the friends of the Cross of Christ.
Love for all peoples, all gifts from the
Father.
Love for all children yet unborn.
Love for the elderly, love for the weak.
Love for the gentle, the lowly, the meek.
Love for the broken-hearted
who weep in the street.
Love for the drug addict who finds no
peace.
Love for the disturbed in mind or emotions.
Love for the possessed, scourged in the
spirit.
Love for the persecutors who secure our
salvation
by driving us deep into the Heart of God.
Love for the single, the married, the rich,
and the poor.
Love for all without reserve.
Love for Love, in Love, with Love.
All becomes one in Love, Love, Love.

The Joy of Suffering
Poem 2

The Joy of Suffering
pain profound.
The Joy of Suffering
...to the cross belong.
The joy of suffering
with Jesus' gown.
In humble resignation
true contemplation.

The cross of suffering
the saints own food.
The cross of humbling
the holy man's good.
The only pleasure,
the cross within.
The joy of suffering
for Jesus' gain.

The joy, O sweet joy,
   when self-love dies.
The life, O sweet life,
   when pride flies.
The death of a sinner
   the life of another.
The ages of suffering
in reparation sacrificing.

O how can this be?—
All is turned backwards.
But backwards was forward
   after the Fall.
Now sing to Jesus
your little song of love.
Love in all suffering
for love shares all out.

Confirmation
Poem 3

Confirmation in the Lord,
new life emerging, order restored.
Confirmation ending all,
beginning all in the All in all.
Confirmation Spiritual birth,
Holy Spirit comes flaming forth.
Confirmation nourishing tide,
ocean of love pouring inside.
Confirmation penance reward,
heavenly food, God's own Word.
Confirmation Father above,
through the raining Flame of Love.
Confirmation heavenly star,
shining emblem, Sun afar.
Confirmation, the cross relieving—
the loss of grace from sensual burdening.
God uniting the soul to His Son,
in the Flame of His Spirit's love.

Winter has ended, summer's come,
the flowers appear in the Summer Sun.
Cool breeze blowing, the Spirit is flowing,
filling the soul to capacity full.
Wounds healed over, tears dried up,
the Banquet table set to sup.
Nakedness covered, a hidden life,
hiding safely as Christ's wife
(spiritually understood).
A bible story, a rosary round,
a circle circled, new life found.

Confirmation glorious crown,
resting quietly in peace profound.
Confirmation white flying Dove,
showering gifts through flaming love.
Confirmation satisfies,
the soul's long longing, sobbing sighs.
Confirmation fortifies,
weak worry warts and wobbling thighs.
Confirmation far spent day,
night is coming, 'watch and pray.'
Confirmation Christ the Lord,
open door to Christ adored.
Confirmation Christ the King,
wedding ring from Christ joining.
Confirmation single-eyed,
lacking nothing as Christ's bride.

Proverbs

(1)
Love opposes
what is contrary to Love.
Hate sin, but not the sinner.

(2)
Be hard on yourself,
but gentle and kind toward others.

(3)
Hate the devil,
and drive him away,
in your spirit, mind, and heart,
by rejecting what disturbs your peace,
and praying to God for the opposite.

(4)
If you don't have a problem,
don't make a problem.

"Sufficient for the day
is the evil thereof."
(Matt. 6:34)

(5)

It is good to be tired,
if required
for the fulfillment of God's will.

(6)

Crosses carry us forward
in the spiritual life
through reparation and purification,
through growth in grace and virtue,
through conformity to Christ Crucified,
Our Model and Our Salvation.

(7)

At every Mass remember
the Real Presence of Jesus Christ
in the Holy Eucharist,
the Glorified Lord, Risen and Real,
whole and entire,
hidden under the appearance of
bread and wine.
Love and adore Him
in your heart and soul and mind.

THE SPIRITUAL LIFE: SOME MORE NOTES

The Spiritual Life: Some More Notes

*They deceive themselves who think that
union with God
consists of
ecstasies and delights in Him.
It consists of nothing else than
the submission of our will,
with our thoughts, words, and actions,
to the will of God.
Union is perfect when the will is detached
from everything
and adheres totally to God in such a manner
that its every movement is nothing other
than the pure will of God.
This is the true and essential union
which I have always desired
and unceasingly asked of God.
—St. Teresa of Avila*

A gradual conversion, turning away from a self-centered worldly way of life to a God-centered Christian way of life, over a period of, say, three months to three years, is more common than a sudden or dramatic conversion such as we see in the life of St. Paul.

At each new level of grace and charity in the spiritual life we need to adjust to a new way of being and of operating in our thoughts, words and deeds that is more Christlike and spiritual, more humble and holy. As the "old man" weakens, withers, and dies inside of us, so, too, do our old ways of thinking, talking and acting that are unChristian or sinful. New ways need to be found and followed, by the grace of God, so that we can grow up in God and become mature Christians, able to follow the inspirations and enlightenments of the Holy Spirit, along with right reason as needed.

"Do not think that I came to bring peace on earth. I came not to bring peace, but the sword." (Matt. 10:34) We cooperate with the grace of God in putting the "old man" to death by using the sword of self-hate to dig out and destroy the sin within us that has been revealed to us by the light of the Holy

Spirit. This self-contempt or self-hate, rightly understood and practiced, is contempt or hate for the "old self" or "old man," the puffed up pride inside of us, the false or phony ego of the "old man" together with its selfish attachments and desires, all of which needs to die in order for the new life of Christ and His Divine grace, the "New Man," to take its place. This "self-hate" may seem extreme or radical, but it is the Gospel. "If any man comes to me, and does not hate his father, and mother, and wife, and children, and brothers, and sisters—yes, even his own life—he cannot be my disciple." (Luke 14:26) Clearly, our relationship with the Lord Jesus Christ must come before all else in the Christian life. Consequently, we are to <u>hate</u> whatever hinders us from fulfilling God's will, whatever weakens or wounds our relationship with God *(whether that be from the devil, the world, or the flesh)*. At the same time, we are to love our neighbor as ourself, which is to love whatever comes from God and leads us to Him, whatever good there is in ourselves or others that can bring us closer to God and help us to be more united to Him, but to hate sin because it separates us from Him.

Pray for what you need in particular, and God will direct you according to His will, either directly, through the inspiration and enlightenment of the Holy Spirit, or through others of good will, or through the circumstances of Divine Providence.

Drive away distractions, as best you can, through Marian prayer and personal confession, and then, continue with your prayer despite the "crown of thorns" you wear, until God lifts it.

The self-examination and active purgation of sin, in cooperation with grace, that is necessary at the beginning of the spiritual life should lead to self-forgetfulness in the presence of God and abandonment to His Holy Will as soon as possible. It is only to make more space for grace, to experience the Divine presence on a deeper level, that we need to root out and remove, as far as we can, the obstacles of sin within. By becoming more like Christ in our thoughts and attitudes, in our practice of charity and virtue and holy desires, we can help prepare the way for the coming of Christ into our lives on a deeper level and in a new way—"Jesus answered and said to him, 'If anyone loves me, he will keep my word, and my Father will love him, and we will come to him, and make our home with him.'" (John 14:23) This indicates a deeper conversion, a spiritual resurrection and the beginning of infused contemplation.

Many times in the spiritual life, God keeps us in the dark, in the sense that He chooses not to reveal more about our spiritual state of soul, of where we are at in the spiritual life, in order to protect us from spiritual pride or vainglory on the one hand, or from undue fear and discouragement on the other. Either way, it is Wisdom Incarnate (Christ the Lord) who leads us. Hold on to Him in your thoughts and desires, in your heart and soul, even when you do not "feel" His presence or "see" Him in the same way as before. When you are ready, when the time is right, He will reveal more to you by the light and love of the Holy Spirit. After the dark night comes the morning sunlight of spiritual freedom and peace in God's presence.

Do not hold on to any particular grace or blessing, but always go beyond it, when you can, to the experience of God as infinite and unknowable, that is to say, to the simple and loving contemplation of God in a general way, in the "cloud of unknowing."

God has no form. We may hear His voice speaking silently in our hearts, but we cannot see Him as He is, in this life. We may know the truth without reasoning, and experience the desire without feeling, but then, we must act in faith on these supernatural illuminations and inspirations from God. The Lord will bless us for obeying His will with an interior peace and spiritual freedom. But when it is not His will, we will know from the dissipation and disorder it causes in the soul and from the suffocating effects of pride and disobedience. It is the difference between dismantling or rebuilding the "old man." The first leads to inner freedom and spiritual spaciousness within the supernatural graciousness of God's presence. The second leads to slavery and confinement within the narrow bounds of the human mind and emotions.

The two parts of "Abandonment to Divine Providence" were perfectly practiced by Our Lady of the Angels, Holy Mary. The passive part is signified by her words at the Incarnation—"Behold, I am the handmaid of the Lord; be it done to me according to your word." (Luke 1:38) The active part is signified by her words to the waiters at the marriage feast—"Do whatever he tells you." (John 2:5)

We deserve nothing, but God has given us everything. It is all a gift of His infinite love, mercy and forgiveness, kindness and goodness. Out of nothing He created everything, and every human person with their own intellect and free will, soul and body. We can take credit for nothing. Whatever good we do, in thought, word or deed, we could not do if we did not exist, and whatever good we do with the help of grace can only come from God's active participation, "for without Me, you can do nothing"—that will bring us closer to God and union with Him, our only true happiness and salvation. (John 15:5) Free will is free, and merits a reward from the Lord for making good choices, but not absolutely. We could not "merit" anything if we did not exist or did not have a spiritual soul with intellect and free will. Good choices made with grace and according to God's will are meritorious not because we deserve it or have it coming in strict justice, but because God has chosen to bless our efforts at cooperating with Him, as is fitting, but not required, strictly speaking. Everything is a gift. All good comes from God, ultimately. Let us praise and thank Him, and in the reality of humility, let us take credit for nothing but our sin, and give God all the honor, glory, praise and thanksgiving—all the credit— for all that is good. He will not fail to fulfill His promises beyond imagining, if we do not fail to love Him to the end, with undaunted and intrepid faith, unrelenting hope, and final perseverance. *"All glory, honor, praise and thanksgiving be to the Most Holy Trinity!—Father, Son, and Holy Spirit, One God, forever and ever. Amen."*

SPIRITUAL SELECTIONS

**Edited and Adapted
by
Orison de Corde**

From—

Manual for Interior Souls
by
John Nicholas Grou

—

***The Spiritual Doctrine of
Father Louis Lallemant***

—

Spiritual Maxims
by
John Nicholas Grou

Truths of the Interior Life

Fundamental Truths of the Interior Life

(Manual for Interior Souls)

*God made me to know Him,
to love Him,
and to serve Him and
to be happy with Him forever
in Heaven.
—Baltimore Catechism*

First Truth

God has only given free will to man that he may consecrate it to Him out of love; therefore, the best use we can make of our free will is to put it in the hands of God again, to renounce all desire to guide ourselves, and to allow God to deal with us in all things as He pleases, because in the designs of God everything that happens to us by the arrangement of His Providence must be for our eternal happiness and salvation.

St. Paul says that—"For those who love God, all things work together for good." (Rom. 8:28) If I govern myself on my own in anything whatever, it is very much to be feared that I shall govern myself badly. "Trust in the Lord with all your heart, and lean not upon your own understanding; in all your ways think of Him, and He will direct your steps." (Proverbs 3:5-6) If I allow myself to be governed by God, however, I am quite sure of being well guided, and that nothing can happen to me that will not be for my greater good, for God loves me infinitely more than I love myself.

God is infinitely wiser and more

enlightened than I am, and if I make Him "my Lord and my God," my Leader and Guide, it is impossible that anything can prevent the execution of His designs of goodness and mercy towards me. This is the first fundamental truth of the interior life.

Second Truth

The second truth is not less certain by experience, and it is this: that the source of the true peace of man is in the gift he makes of himself to God, and that when this gift *(as far as possible)* is full and entire, generous, complete and irrevocable, the peace which he will enjoy in his heart and soul will likewise be uninterrupted, and will increase and be strengthened from one day to another even by events which apparently might change it or do it harm. The only happiness in life, the only happiness we can obtain for ourselves by the good use of our free will, is peace of heart, by the mercy and grace of God. And this peace is not for the wicked, as God tells us in Holy Scripture. (Isaiah 48:22) The peace also of those half-hearted Christians who have not fully given themselves to God is very weak, very tottering, very much troubled either by the scruples of their conscience or their fear of the judgements of God, or the various accidents and events of life. When is it then that a deep, solid, and unchangeable peace takes root in a soul? From the moment that it gives itself entirely to God it enters into a rest and a peace that is none other than the peace of God Himself, upon whom it leans. We share, necessarily, in the nature of the things to which we attach ourselves. If I unite myself to things that are continually in motion, I experience the same agitation myself; if I unite myself to God, who alone is unchangeable, I share in His immutability, and nothing can shake me so long as I do not separate myself from Him *(by taking my will back from Him again in order to pursue my own will).*

Third Truth

We are not capable, of ourselves, either of great or little things for God; but we must rather desire little things, leaving it to God, when He thinks fit, to make us do great things.

Little opportunities of serving and loving

Him present themselves every day, almost every instant—great ones rarely offer themselves to us. Little things conduce no less to our sanctification than great ones, and perhaps they even do so more, because they keep us humble, and give self-love *(pride)* nothing to feed upon. Fidelity in little things, a carefulness to please God in all things, even small things, proves the reality and the delicacy of our love for Him. We may do little things with such an exalted motive *(purely for God)* that they may be more pleasing to the Blessed Trinity than the greatest things done in less perfect dispositions. Let us cast an eye upon the holy house of Nazareth, and the simple and wonderful lives led there, and we shall be convinced of the truth of this. Finally, one thing is certain by the teaching of Holy Scripture, and that is that they who neglect and despise little things, of which they were obliged, will also neglect greater ones. (Luke 16:10) Let us then aspire to the perfect practice of little things and of the duty of the present moment, of abandonment to divine providence and docility to the Holy Spirit, of child-like simplicity and humble and loving charity, of peaceful prayer in the presence of God.

Fourth Truth

The love of God has in us only one enemy, which is the love of self, in other words, pride or self-centeredness. The devil is only strong against us, and only has power over us, through this pride or self-love. Human respect *(the desire to please others for selfish reasons, such as, to protect our pride or receive worldly favors)*, which is so terribly strong in so many souls, is the child of self-love. All the obstacles we meet with, all the interior disturbances we experience, come only from self-love *(our own pride and selfishness)*. Moreover, in proportion as self-love is weakened and dissolved, and we give up our own judgement and bend our own will to the will of God—which is the honor and glory of God and His good pleasure—so will our difficulties be overcome, our conflicts will cease, our troubles will vanish, and peace and calm will be established in our hearts. Self-love *(Pride)*, which at first is open and vulgar and plainly seen becomes more delicate and more spiritual as we advance in the spiritual life. And the more spiritual it is, and the deeper and more secret it is, so much the more difficult is it to uproot, and so much the more distress and agony of spirit does it cost us to deliver ourselves from it.

We only know self-love, we can only see our pride, as far as the Divine light reveals it to us, and God only shows it to us by degrees, in proportion as He wishes to destroy it; thus, self-love *(pride)* is only known to us by the blows that God deals at it and that we deal at it conjointly with God, and gradually Divine love occupies the place from which self-love *(the false and phony ego of the "old man")* has been driven, until at last Divine love succeeds in driving it completely from the center of the soul, and reigns there alone, without a rival. When once a soul belongs to Divine love fully, it is perfectly purified; it may still have to suffer, but it resists no more, and it enjoys the most profound peace in the midst of its suffering.

Let us follow the different states of the spiritual life, and let us see in a general manner, without going into details, how God pursues self-love *(pride)* from place to place in each of these states.

The most gross kind of self-love *(pride)* manifests itself in the senses, and in the attachment to the things of sense. The "pride of life" is derived from the "life of the senses" or the strength of sensuality. (1 John 2:16) God drives it out by purifying the senses with His own sweetness and with heavenly consolations, which inspire the soul with a desire for God and the things of God along with a disgust and contempt for all sinful worldly pleasures and pursuits. (Matt. 6:24)

Then self-love *(self-seeking)* attaches itself to these consolations, to this peace, to this feeling of recollection, until God takes away that support, and withdraws little by little all sense and feeling, leaving to the soul, at the same time, its peace and tranquility.

At last, by various kinds of trials, He seemingly disturbs this peace upon which self-love was relying. We begin to lose ground, and to find no longer any resource in ourselves.

Then to the trials which come from God are joined the temptations of the devil. We find ourselves stained with thoughts against purity, against faith and hope and charity; then we begin no longer to rely on our own strength or our own virtue; we think ourselves stained with sin even when we have not consented to the suggestions of the devil. The temptations are always increasing, and our resistance, I do not say really, but apparently, is always growing weaker, in such manner that at last we imagine we have consented; we see ourselves covered with sins, and for this reason we imagine ourselves rejected by God and forsaken by Him; it is now that self-love *(pride)* is really desolate, and finds the greatest difficulty in serving God for Himself alone, without any consolation. This state lasts until we have learned to seek not ourselves *(our own will and pleasure)* but the good pleasure of God and His will in all things, despite the difficulty. Then self-love *(pride)* dies to the degree that God wills and we are filled, commensurately full, with greater grace and charity, humility and spiritual freedom, peace and presence of God, joy and the Holy Spirit, infused contemplation and interior recollection.

This process of purification will be repeated, years later, for those who go on to perfection, but it will take place at the deepest and highest level of the spiritual life—to the utter destruction of self-love and the "old man," and to the transforming union of the soul with God, through Christ our Lord. What then follows is perfect peace and freedom, spiritual recollection and contemplation, the Living Flame of Love, nourishing and satisfying, the life of Christ and union, the mystery of the Trinity and wisdom, the grace of God and mercy, the love of God and neighbor, the angels and saints of heaven and participation, the end of time's urgency and the beginning of eternity.

Fifth Truth

In the whole course of the sanctification of a soul, the action of God steadily increases, and the action of the soul itself steadily grows less, until at last all its care is to let go of its own activity in order to place no obstacle in the way of the Divine operation. The soul then becomes gradually more passive, and God exercises His power in, with and through it more and more, until the will of the creature is united entirely with the will of God and transformed in Christ our Lord.

The great point, therefore, when we have once given ourselves to God completely, is to allow ourselves to be despoiled of every obstacle to His grace, for the Lord Jesus Christ will only fill the soul that has freely given up its own will—and only to the degree that it is free of selfish attachments and the spirit of possessiveness. "When the young man heard this word, he went away sad, for he had many possessions." (Matt. 19:20) A love which counts the cost, which calculates, which looks at its own interest, in a word which will go only so far and no farther, is not a perfect love. To be truly worthy of God, a love must be without measure and without bounds; it must rise above human reason and prudence, and must go as far as folly, even the folly of the cross! It is so that our Lord and Savior Jesus Christ loved His Father; it is so that He loves each one of us. Let us love Him thus in return, without holding anything back, and we will be filled, ever more fully, with His Divinity, by being united to His Sacred Humanity.

On The Means of Attaining Virtue

(Manual for Interior Souls)

*It is just (fitting) that He should act with reserve towards those who act with reserve towards Him.
On the contrary,
He gives Himself entirely to those souls, who, driving from their hearts everything that is not God,
and does not lead to love of Him,
and giving themselves to Him without reserve, truly say to Him— 'My God and my All!'*
—St. Alphonsus de Liguori

The first means of attaining virtue, which seems the most easy, and is in reality the most difficult, is to <u>will</u> it; but with a sincere, entire, efficacious, and constant will. And oh how rare is this *good will!* We imagine we will a thing, but in truth and reality we do not will it at all. We may have desires, longings, purposes, wishes; but that is not having a strong and determined will. We wish to be devout (sincere Christians), but in our own way up to a certain point, and provided it does not cost us too much. We wish, and we are contented with wishing. We do not carry our wishes into practice; we are discouraged as soon as it is necessary to put our hand to the work, to overcome obstacles or set them aside, to fight against our faults, to struggle with (fallen) nature and all its evil propensities. We wish to-day perhaps; we begin bravely, but alas! our energies are soon relaxed. We undertake, and then we give up. We do not want to see that everything depends upon perseverance. "No man putting his hand to the plough, and looking back, is fit for the kingdom of God." (Luke 9:62)

Let us ask God to grant us this *good will;* let us ask Him for it every day; and by our fidelity to the grace of today, let us try to continue in it, intent upon doing His will.

The second means is to follow a regular routine of spiritual exercises, such as morning and evening prayer, nightly examination of conscience, quiet time alone with God together with spiritual reading.

The third means is to try and realize always the presence of God. To attain this, we must know that, as converted Christians, God is with us in our inmost heart and soul. We will find Him there, if we seek Him, for God inspires holy thoughts and good desires, the interior inclination to do good and the salutary aversion to evil. It is the voice of God Himself who warns us, reproves us, enlightens us, and directs us. The great thing is always to be attentive and faithful to this voice *(of the Holy Spirit)* within us. It is not in dissipation, nor in the agitation and tumult of the world, that we shall hear it; but in solitude, in peace, in the silence of our passions and imaginations. The greatest step towards perfection which someone can make, is to keep himself habitually in such a state that he can always hear the voice of God, when He speaks; to endeavor to possess himself in peace, to avoid everything that may distract him *(from the will of God)*, everything that makes him uneasy, everything to which he is inordinately attached. All this must be for a long time the subject of a particular examination of conscience and a continual struggle.

The fourth means is to give specially to God a certain time in the day, when we can occupy ourselves with Him alone, and with the thought of His presence; when we can speak to Him, not with our lips, but in the depths of our heart, and listen to what He has to say to us. This is what is called mental prayer *(as distinguished from vocal prayer)*. To facilitate these "quiet times," we can make use of a book, such as *The Imitation of Christ*, making a pause at each verse or section while meditating and trying to understand the spiritual doctrine it contains. At first we may give to this exercise a quarter of an hour a day; but we should gradually accustom ourselves to spend at least one half hour a day on this spontaneous personal prayer, this interior prayer of the heart, which may, at times, express itself in vocal prayer besides. As we develop a taste for mental prayer, and can carry it on without a book, we may from time to time keep ourselves peacefully in the simple presence of God, recollected in Him, and begging of Him to act upon our soul, and to do with it according to His good pleasure. It is a great error to consider as idleness or waste of time the moments which we pass thus, keeping ourselves recollected and attentive before God, whether He pleases or not to make us sensible of His action on our soul, provided we continue to have the interior inclination to silence and solitude in the peace of God's presence.

The fifth means of acquiring true and solid virtue is frequently to approach the sacraments, which are the principal sources of grace. We must not make a torment of Confession; that would be quite against the intention of God; neither must we make of it a mere matter of routine without the honest effort at reform and conversion. The things of which persons who are striving after perfection ought chiefly to accuse themselves are sinful actions *(in word or deed)*, willing omissions of some necessary good, and sinful desires that have been consented to since their last Confession. The spiritual person may also add the feelings of puffed up pride to which they have yielded, the greed or gluttony they have indulged in, and the lights from God they have resisted or ignored, causing a loss of grace and peace and good order. The reception of Holy Communion is always well made when we come from it with renewed courage and a fresh resolution to be more faithful to God than ever. We must not think, that to make a good Confession and Communion we must necessarily make use of all the prayers and practices which are to be found in the back of church books or pamphlets. To follow a written guideline is certainly a good method for young people, whose imagination is generally quick and lively, or for those who have been away from the sacraments for some time, or, generally, for those who are new to the spiritual life. But when we have once become familiar with these methods and have entered resolutely on the way of prayer, we need no longer go to books or pamphlets for help, either to receive Holy Communion or for Confession. The Holy Spirit will enlighten and inspire us as to our method of preparation and participation; and yet, this may well still include some of those earlier prayers and practices.

The sixth means is spiritual reading; and we must be very careful in the choice of books. As a rule, we should prefer to all others those which touch the heart and carry with them a certain unction of the

Holy Spirit which is not to be mistaken. <u>*The Spiritual Combat*</u> by Dom Lorenzo Scupoli is one such example, and a spiritual classic that may be read with profit by beginners, as well as those more advanced in the spiritual life. Here is an excerpt, with some adaptations, from that esteemed work: "The first thing you are to do when you awake, is to open the eyes of your soul, and consider yourself as in the field of battle, facing the enemy, and under an absolute necessity of engaging or perishing forever. Know that before you is the enemy, that particular vice or disorderly passion you are endeavoring to subdue according to your intention of practicing the opposite virtue from the evening examination of conscience the night before. Imagine that it is a hideous monster coming to devour you. At the same time, remember and represent to yourself Jesus Christ, your invincible leader, attended by the Blessed Virgin, St. Joseph, and a vast array of Angels and Saints, including the glorious Archangel St. Michael. On the other hand, behold the Devil and his troops ready to support that passion or vice you contend with and who are resolved to leave nothing undone to accomplish your downfall.

Listen to your Guardian Angel who exhorts you to the practice of virtue with words such as these: 'This day you must exert yourself in order to subdue your enemy, and all who seek your ruin. Take courage, let no vain fears or apprehensions seize you, since Christ your Captain is near at hand with all the power of Heaven to protect you against all enemies and to prevent their ever reducing you, either by force or treachery, under their subjection. Maintain your ground, use violence with yourself, whatever pain it may occasion; call aloud on Jesus and Mary; beg the assistance of all the Angels and Saints; do some spiritual reading; and this being done, depend upon God for gaining the victory.' Thus, as we advance in grace and virtue, the difficulties which at first occurred after our conversion, continually diminish, and a certain delight with which God is pleased to sweeten the bitterness of this life, increases in proportion. Thus, going cheerfully *(gratefully)* on from virtue to virtue by receiving 'grace upon grace,' we reach at last the mountaintop, the height of Christian perfection, that happy state, wherein the soul begins to practice virtue, not only without disgust, but with

MEANS OF ATTAINING VIRTUE · 67

unspeakable interior pleasure and spiritual delight. Triumphant as she is over her passions, the world, and herself, she lives in God, and through Him, amidst her continual labors of love and service, enjoys an undisturbed peace and inner tranquility."

Our spiritual reading, furthermore, should be half a prayer; that is to say, that in reading we should listen for the voice of God speaking to us in some way through this reading, and stop to meditate *(pause and consider it)* when we feel ourselves touched by what we read. We ought to read with a view to practice what we read; and as everything does not suit everybody, we should seek what is most in accordance with our own needs, and follow its teachings faithfully, always taking care not to multiply our practices of devotion too much, for that is fatal to liberty of spirit (and abandonment to God's will), which we should always try to preserve.

The seventh means of attaining virtue is the mortification of the heart *(through prayer—especially, The Four Step Prayer— self-denial, and abandonment to God's will)*. Everything within us *(of the "old man")* is opposed to our supernatural good;

everything still fallen draws us towards the slavery of the senses and of self-love *(self-centeredness, pride and selfishness)*. We must struggle continually against ourselves, and wage a constant war against our own inclinations, either in resisting impressions from without or fighting with those from within. We cannot watch too much over our own heart to see what it is inclined to, what it desires, what it is attached to, and all that passes there. This is painful in the beginning; but it becomes easy as we grow accustomed to retiring into ourselves for prayer and recollection and keeping ourselves in the presence of God.

The eighth means is a true devotion to the holy Angels and Saints of God, especially to the Blessed Virgin Mary and our Guardian Angel. Let us ask through Holy Mary of Jesus Christ, her Son, the grace and help we need so much, and she will most certainly obtain them for us. Above all things, when we are tempted to disgust, to weariness, to discouragement, to a feeling that we would like to give up trying to be good altogether, let us fly to her with a holy confidence that she can and will help us.

As regards our Guardian Angel, let us

remember that he never leaves us and that he has been given to us by God, to guide us in the way of holiness. Let us speak to him in all our doubts, in all our difficulties, and let us often ask him to watch over and protect us, addressing him reverently as "Holy Angel of God" or "Guardian Angel of God" or suchlike, without seeking to know his name in particular *(which could lead to confusion or deception).* (Genesis 32:29)

Finally, the most important point is to have a good spiritual guide, a director, teacher or advisor well versed in the ways of God, and who is himself or herself led by the Spirit of God. These good directors have always been very rare, and today they are more so than ever. Nevertheless, if a converted Christian is determined to grow closer to God— to do His will and not their own—and earnestly prays that they may find someone who can help them to do this, they will unfailingly find the right person by the providence of God. Yet, because not everyone can be "all things to all men," they may need others also, who can help them to grow in the spiritual life, or even go from one director to another if the circumstances of divine providence call for that. (1 Cor. 9:22) Rarely, do we find someone who has both knowledge and experience of the spiritual life in great measure, but insofar as they are familiar with the ways of God, humble and holy, we can entrust the direction of our soul to them. Let us, then, open our heart and soul to them, listen to their advice with docility, and follow it, as far as we can, in meekness and humility. If they are the one God has chosen to lead us, they will reveal His will to us as if God spoke to us through them. A soul with the right dispositions and well guided by one who is filled with the Holy Spirit and divine wisdom—by one who has "the mind of Christ" as revealed in the Gospel and in the saints—can never fail to attain sanctity. (Phil. 2:5-11)

(The following is from, <u>The Spiritual Doctrine of Father Louis Lallemant</u>) Two extremes must be avoided in the direction of spiritual persons. One is, giving too easy credence and confirmation to the experience of souls who, having read about the marvelous and mystical operations of grace in the saints, imagine they are already being favored with the like when they experience the least sensible sweetnesses in their prayer life. Dangerous vanity! that can easily lead to spiritual pride. The other

is, keeping souls down too low when God is calling them to higher things. There are directors who will not listen to any mention of contemplation, or heavenly visitations, or extraordinary favors, because they themselves have not experienced them. This is also prejudicial to the advancement of souls in the spiritual life. "Do not quench the Spirit"—either by overrating *(thereby, inducing pride)* or by discounting *(thereby, causing doubt, fear or discouragement)* genuine spiritual experiences of God's grace and divine presence. (1 Thes. 5:19)

On the Violence We Must Use To Die to Ourselves

(Manual for Interior Souls)

Be as eager to break your own will as the thirsty stag is to drink of the refreshing waters.
—St. Paul of the Cross

"From the days of John the Baptist, even until now," said our Lord and Savior Jesus Christ, "the kingdom of Heaven has been subject to violence, and the violent take it by force." (Matt. 11:12)

If, in one sense Jesus Christ has rendered the way to Heaven more easy, by the abundant outpouring of His grace, and by the spirit of love with which He has filled His disciples; on the other hand, He has made this way even more narrow and difficult, because He came to fulfill the law *(of love)* in its perfection, and, as grace is more readily and abundantly available since His coming, He requires more from His followers than God required formerly under the law of nature *(natural law)* and the law of Moses. Thus, from the moment when John the Baptist announced the coming of the Savior, the kingdom of Heaven was to be obtained through the violence we do to ourselves; we must seize it and take it by force. This saying is hard to our fallen nature, because it is against fallen nature itself that we must do battle and wage war, and this resistance must sometimes be "unto blood," without truce or compromise. If the service of God and Christian perfection consisted only in a certain routine of external devotion, compatible with a life of ease and comfort, with all the allurements of self-indulgence, and with a secret self-esteem in ourselves and self-satisfaction in all we do, the number of saintly souls—that is to say, true Christians, true lovers of the Gospel— would not be so rare. But as it is, Jesus

Christ has, to a great extent, replaced the exterior practices of the Mosaic Law with interior ones, which are far more difficult and painful as also the grace given is far greater and more abundant, "For the law was given through Moses; but grace and truth came through Jesus Christ." (John 1:17)

Our Lord said, "Do not think that I have come to bring peace on earth. I came not to bring peace, but the sword." (Matt. 10:34) He puts this sword *(which is a "good will")* in the hands of His servants, and He wishes that they should make use of it against themselves, in that circumcision of the heart which mortifies without pity all the corrupt inclinations of their fallen nature (for example, to puffed up pride, impurity, greed or anger), even to finally putting them to death, and leaving in the heart, thus mortified, no single trace of the old Adam.

Oh! what a great and difficult work is this total destruction, this total annihilation, of the selfish and self-centered creature, the false and deceitful old Adam, the sin within—the "old man!" Again I say, how hard, how difficult to bear this! So long as it is only a question of saying certain prescribed prayers, of visiting the church, of practicing works of charity, plenty of people can be found to embrace this kind of devotion. A spiritual leader who requires no more than this is eagerly listened to: he is a man of God; he is a saint. But if he begins to speak of correcting certain defects, of overcoming human respect *(seeking to please man instead of God)*, of reforming natural character *(the disordered or inordinate aspects thereof)*, of keeping a check on natural inclinations and feelings, and of following in everything the leading of grace, he is no longer listened to; he is exaggerating, he is going beyond all bounds!

It is nevertheless certain that the true spirit of Christianity consists in this: that a real Christian should look upon himself as his greatest enemy; that he should wage continual war against himself; that he should spare himself in nothing, and count all his progress by the victories he gains over himself.

When we begin to give ourselves entirely to God, He treats us at first with great clemency, to win us to Himself. He fills the soul with an ineffable peace and joy *(known as the "first fervor")*. He causes us to delight in solitude, in recollection, and in all our religious duties. He makes the practice of virtue easy to us; nothing is a trouble to us. We think we are capable of everything.

But as soon as He is certain of a man, immediately God begins to enlighten him as to his defects; He raises by degrees the veil which concealed them from him, and He inspires him with a firm will to overcome them. From that moment such a man turns against himself; he undertakes the conquest of self-love *(pride);* he pursues it relentlessly wherever he perceives it; and when he is thoroughly illuminated by the Divine light, where does he *not* perceive it? He sees in himself nothing but misery, imperfection, and sin; self-seeking and attachment to his own will; his very devotion appears to him full of defects. He once thought he loved God, and now he finds that this love was largely but another form of self-seeking; that he has appropriated to himself the gifts of God *(through spiritual pride or spiritual gluttony);* that he has served God almost entirely for selfish ends; that he has thought highly of himself and despised others whom he considers not to have received the same graces as himself.

God shows him all this gradually; for if

He were to show it to him all at once he could not bear it, and would fall into despair. But the little He does show him is sufficient to convince him that he has many and many a hard battle to fight before he can arrive at the end of it.

If a man is courageous and faithful, what does he then do? He humbles himself, without despairing; he places all his confidence in God; he implores His assistance in the war he is going to undertake. Then, he fills his mind and heart with this spiritual maxim from <u>The Imitation of Christ</u>—"The greater violence you do to your *(old)* self, the greater progress shall you make... For there a man makes greater progress and merits greater grace where he overcomes himself the more and mortifies *(empties/humbles)* himself in spirit *(by self-sacrifice, prayer and penance)."* Here is the purest spirit of the Gospel which all of the saints have followed.

After their example, this man declares war against his fallen nature, against his own thoughts and desires, against his sinful tendencies and vices, including those of the body, along with his soul, "I chastise my body, and bring it under subjection *(to the inspirations of the Holy Spirit and to the practice of virtue),* lest after preaching to others, I myself should be disqualified." (1 Cor. 9:27) And in order to avoid getting bogged down in scrupulosity or carried away with an impatient or indiscreet zeal, he begs of God that He may Himself direct him and protect him in this battle against the "old man."

Now he is a true soldier of Jesus Christ; now he is enrolled under His banner *(the cross)*—"If any one will come after me, let him deny himself, take up his cross daily, and follow me." (Luke 9:23) Until now God has only been preparing and disposing him for this great grace; but from this moment he is clothed with the armor of faith, and enters in good earnest upon the field of battle.

How long shall this conflict last?

It shall last as long as there is one enemy to conquer, as long as there is one obstacle in the soul to be overcome, in other words, it shall last until the "old man," the old Adam, is utterly dead and destroyed and nothing.

A good Christian never lays down his arms, and all is not finished for him even when he has fought until his strength is exhausted. What do I mean to say by this? What can remain for him to do when he is worn-out by his own victories, and when he has carried his violence against himself as far as it can possibly go? There remains nothing for him to do, but there remains for him to suffer the action of God, who henceforth will do alone what is beyond the strength of man.

In the beginning of the spiritual life, our sanctification is the work of our own efforts, sustained and assisted by Divine grace: it is finished and perfected solely by the Divine operation. Man raises the edifice *(of virtue)* as high as he can, but because there is still a great deal that is merely human *(and not supernatural)* in this edifice *(namely, human ego and pride)*, God destroys all the work of man, and substitutes for it His own work; and the creature has nothing else to do but to allow the Creator to act as He pleases. The creature acts no more *(or very little)*, but he suffers, because God (who is Purity) is acting upon him (who is corruption). This is the passive purification of the soul *(in both the night of the senses and the night of the spirit)*. All the work of God then consists in destroying, in overturning, in despoiling the soul, and reducing it to emptiness, nakedness of spirit. All that is required of us at this time is to patiently allow ourselves to be despoiled of all the gifts, all the graces, all the virtues with which God had adorned us, and which we had subtly appropriated to ourselves. From the consciousness of strength which comes from the life of the senses, we are secretly filled with self-love and pride; we feel we are partly responsible for the good we do by the grace of God. After we have been raised from the life of the senses to the life of the spirit—through the dark night of the senses and, most especially, through the dark night of the spirit, where God's "power is made perfect in weakness"—we can humbly, yet truly say, "I have strength for all things, in Christ who strengthens me." (2 Cor. 12:9)(Phil. 4:13)

"Thanks be to Thee, infinite Mercy! You have begun the work of setting me free of the old Adam; and my ardent hope is that You will continue it and finish it. I wish to have no other part in it than to co-operate with You as much as I am able, and then to let go and let You do with me as You will. Amen."

On the Annihilation of Self

(Manual for Interior Souls)

> *Attribute to God,*
> *and not to self,*
> *whatever good one sees in oneself;*
> *but know that the evil in oneself*
> *comes only from self.*
> —St. Benedict

When we are spoken to of dying to ourselves, of annihilating ourselves, when we are told that that is the foundation of Christian morality, and that in it consists the adoration of God in spirit and in truth, we do not wish to accept the statement; it seems to us hard and even unjust *(too radical or extreme)*, and we rebel against those who announce it to us on the part of God. Let us convince ourselves once for all that this saying has nothing but what is just and right in itself, and that the practice of it is infinitely sweeter than we think. Afterwards let us humble ourselves if we have not the courage to put it in practice; and instead of condemning the words of wisdom, let us condemn ourselves... For God requires of us nothing but what is reasonable, having created us out of nothing for Himself alone.

In all contempt or calumnies we may have to suffer, in all humiliations, interior or exterior, that we undergo, the thing which really hurts us and really makes them hard to bear is our own pride; it is because we wish to be esteemed and considered, and treated with a certain respect, and that we do not at all like the idea of being treated with ridicule and contempt by others, or seen as less than perfect by ourselves. This is what really agitates us, and makes us indignant, and renders our life bitter and insupportable. Let us set seriously to work to annihilate ourselves, let us give no food to pride, let us put away from us all the first movements of self-esteem and self-love, and let us accept patiently and even joyfully, in the depth of our soul, all the little mortifications which come to us. Little by little we shall come to not caring in the very least about what is thought of us or said of us, or how we are treated. A person who is dead to his ego and pride feels nothing inside that can be disturbed; for him there is no more concern about honor or reputation; praise and blame are equal and the same to him. There is nothing in heaven, or on earth, or in hell, that can trouble the peace of a soul that is truly annihilated *(dead to himself, his own self-will).*

I may add that this way of annihilation, against which human nature in our fallen state cries out so strongly, is not really so painful as we imagine, and it is even sweet. For, first of all, our Lord and Savior Jesus Christ has said so—"Take My yoke upon you," He says, "for it is sweet and light." (Matt. 11:29-30) However heavy this yoke *(of obedience to God's will)* may be in itself, God will lighten it for those who willingly take it up, and who consent to bear it for the love of Him.

On the Human Heart

(Manual for Interior Souls)

*More perverse than all else is the human heart,
and exceedingly corrupt—
who can know it?
—Jeremiah 17:9*

As a consequence of the original sin—the giving in to the Serpent's temptation—the human heart has fallen down from its original uprightness, has been taken from God and given to creatures, especially, to our own selves. Therefore, we must return our free will back to God—give our heart to Him once again (as in <u>The Four Step Prayer</u>)—to begin to undo the damage done, to free our heart and soul and mind from the venom of self-love, the poison of pride, and the muck and mire of unruly passions.

The source of all our vices and the fundamental obstacle to receiving God's graces—is this reversal of the right order of things.

The seeds of this disorder in our fallen human nature take root and make serious progress even before the age of reason. Consequently, all of our actions, even the best of them, have something of this self-centered self-love or pride in them, which deprives them, proportionately, of some of their goodness. And the saddest thing about the whole matter is that the first effect of this disorder is to blind us as to our own state of sinfulness; we can see the faults of others plainly enough, but we cannot and will not see our own. We do all we possibly can to hide what we really are from ourselves and from others. We do not always succeed with others, who generally find us out; but, unfortunately, we succeed only too well with ourselves; and the knowledge of our own hearts, which is the most necessary of all knowledge, remains also the most rare, and that which we take the least trouble to obtain, sometimes laboring all our lives to disguise ourselves in our own eyes. What a terrible mistake, when we have to appear at last before the

God of truth, there at last to see ourselves as we really are! Only then, it will be too late to repent or convert.

If, however, while still in this life, we humbly acknowledge before God our own blindness with regard to ourselves, most assuredly He will enlighten us; and if we will only make good use of these first rays of His Divine light, we shall see more and more clearly, day by day, into our own hearts; we shall discover by degrees all our defects, even those most imperceptible; even the cunning deceits of self-love *(prideful self-centeredness or self-seeking)* will not be able to escape from our vision; and, by the Divine assistance, we shall pursue this enemy of true love relentlessly until we succeed, by the grace of God, in banishing him *(the "old man")* for ever from our hearts. "The soul can know clearly whether or not she loves God purely. If she loves Him, her heart or love will not be set on herself or her own satisfaction and gain, but upon pleasing God and giving Him honor and glory. In the measure she loves herself *(her own will and desire)* that much less she loves God." (St. John of the Cross)

The most important point is, therefore, to walk always under the guidance of the

Divine light *(coming to us directly or through others);* to be quite sure that, if we wander away from that light, we shall lose our spiritual life; to mistrust our own intellect, our own judgement, our own opinion, and to be guided in everything by the Spirit of God; to wait for His decision, and to hold our own in suspense until He decides for us and directs us. How rare is such a practice as this, and what great fidelity in mortifying ourselves it requires! But also, by it, what errors we avoid, what falls we escape, what progress we make in the way of perfection!

What errors we avoid! It is quite certain that whenever we judge of the things of God *(religious or spiritual things)* by our own judgement, we are at fault; that we deceive ourselves in everything respecting the nature of holiness and the means of attaining it; that we are as incapable of judging of our own actions, our own motives, our own dispositions, as we are of the actions and dispositions of our neighbor; that in him as in ourselves we condemn where we ought to approve, and approve what we ought to condemn, on slight grounds and without any knowledge of the true state of things. And as our judgements on such matters are the principles of our conduct, into what errors do not we fall when we take the promptings of our own human mind and spirit for our guide! We construct our own ideal of sanctity; we are quite delighted with it; then, we judge ourselves and we judge others by this self-made rule. How far from true sanctity is this!—that is, from a sanctity which consists in being "poor in spirit," humble of heart, and full of burning charity, ever given to God's will and not our own, in faith and hope and loving abandonment.

What falls we escape! All our faults come from leaving the Spirit of God to follow our own spirit. We are not sufficiently careful about this in the beginning; we do not mistrust ourselves enough; we do not always consult God with the deepest humility; instead, we lean upon our own strength and spirit, our own mind and imagination, and imagine that we are following the Divine Light when it is, rather, our own thought and desire. But then, we fall into sin, temptation, or other difficulties which are of our own making. Here, God is calling us back to Himself, and—if we are humble enough and willing—we can repent and repair the damage done, we can learn from our mistakes and get back on track, we can return to Him with greater humility and loving wisdom—by letting go of our own will and ideas and giving ourselves over, once again, to the will of God—abandoning ourselves into the hands of Divine Providence and the guidance of the Holy Spirit, which brings peace and order.

There is only one way of making real progress in the way of perfection, and that is, never to guide ourselves, but always to take God for our Guide, to renounce ourselves in all things, to die to ourselves, to our own judgement and to our own will. The moment we attempt to guide ourselves we go backwards in the spiritual life; and the farther we advance, the more absolutely necessary is the Divine guidance for us... Can we do better than to place all our conduct in God's hands, and to beg of Him to guide us in all things, that we may do simply, and humbly, and peacefully, whatever He puts into our heart to do? As long as a man that is determined to follow Jesus Christ in all things is at peace in his inmost depths, he may be quite certain that Jesus Christ is guiding and directing him.

On the Guidance of the Holy Spirit

(The Spiritual Doctrine)

*You could not love Jesus
if you did not possess the living source
of holy and pure love,
namely, the Holy Spirit.
Our divine Redeemer said,
'He that believes in Me,
out of his belly
shall flow rivers of living water.
Now this He said of the Spirit
which they were to receive
who believed in Him.'
Therefore,*

> *when God enkindles in you*
> *the flames of divine love,*
> *holy, pure, and without stain,*
> *let yourself disappear*
> *in the infinite Good,*
> *and, like an infant,*
> *sleep the sleep of faith and love*
> *in the arms of your*
> *heavenly Spouse.*
> —St. Paul of the Cross

When a soul has given itself up to the leading of the Holy Spirit, He raises it little by little, and directs it. At the first it knows not where it is going; but gradually the interior light illuminates it, and enables it to behold all its own actions, and the guidance of God therein, so that it has scarcely anything else to do than to let God work in it and by it whatever He pleases; thus it makes wonderful progress in the ways of God, growing closer to Him in the spiritual life, and being of benefit to others as well.

<u>The principal means by which we come to this direction of the Holy Spirit are:</u>

To obey faithfully God's will so far as we know it, though much of it is hidden from us, for we are full of ignorance. By making good use of the knowledge we do have of the will of God, He will give us more light and truth over time, along with the desire and inspiration to fulfill it. Let us fulfill His will—God's designs for our life—so far as He has made it known to us, and He will gradually manifest His providential plan more fully by the light and love of the Holy Spirit.

To renew often the good resolution of following the will of God in all things, and to strengthen this intention in our mind and heart.

To ask God to help us to do His will, by following the Holy Spirit in all things.

To watch with care the different movements of our heart and soul and mind. By such attention we shall gradually come to perceive, by the light of the Holy Spirit, what is of God and what is not. That which proceeds from God in the depths of a soul which is in a state of grace, is peaceable and calm. That which comes from the devil is violent *(causing agitation)*, and brings with it trouble and anxiety.

Other Important Considerations Concerning the Guidance of the Holy Spirit:

"Without *(supernatural)* faith it is impossible to please God." (Heb. 11:6) In order to please God and fulfill His will, we need faith in God and in the supernatural guidance of the Holy Spirit coming to us directly or through others who are guided by the Holy Spirit.

"But when He, the Spirit of truth, comes, He will guide you into all truth." (John 16:13) The guidance which we receive from the Holy Spirit, by means of His gifts, presupposes the faith and authority of the Church, acknowledges them as its rule, admits nothing which is contrary to them, and aims only at uniting us to Christ and His Mystical Body—the Catholic Church—by the exercise of faith and the other virtues.

"The Paraclete *(Advocate, Counselor, Comforter)*, the Holy Spirit, whom the Father will send in my name, He will teach you all things, and bring all things to your mind, whatsoever I have said to you." (John 14:26) The gift of the Holy Spirit—in full measure—was given to the Church on

Pentecost Sunday, and in particular, to the Apostles of Jesus Christ our Lord. Consequently, it is only in and through the Catholic Church that we can receive the fullness of the Holy Spirit and the means of salvation, individual sinners, whether priests or laity, notwithstanding.

Furthermore, just as the interior inspiration of grace coming from the Holy Spirit does not set aside the assent which we give to the articles of faith, as they are externally proposed to us *(eg., in the Nicene Creed)* but, on the contrary, gently disposes the understanding to believe; so also, the guidance which we receive from the gifts of the Holy Spirit, far from interfering with obedience to religious superiors, aids and facilitates the practice of it. Therefore, all this interior guidance, and even divine *(private)* revelations, must always be subordinate to obedience to Church authority; in speaking of the guidance of the Holy Spirit, this tacit condition is ever implied: that obedience to the Church enjoins nothing to the contrary.

Therefore, in the state of faith in which we live, we ought to make more account of the commandment of our superior than of that which our Lord Himself might have given us by an immediate revelation, because we are assured that it is His will we should act in this matter after the pattern of the saints, who by submitting to obedience merited to be raised to a higher reward than they would have been had they paid exclusive regard to the revelations they received.

The only fear is lest superiors should sometimes follow too much the suggestions of human prudence, and for want of discernment condemn the lights and inspirations of the Holy Spirit, treating them as dreams or illusions, and prescribing for those to whom God communicates Himself by supernatural favors of this kind, as if they were sick patients.

If such is the case, we must still obey; but in His own time God will know how to correct the error of these rash persons, and teach them to their cost, not to condemn His graces without understanding them, and without being competent to pronounce upon them.

What renders these particular religious superiors incapable of forming a right judgment is, that they live entirely in external things and in the hurry of business, and have but little spirituality about them, never having risen above the lowest degrees of mental prayer. And what induces them to pass judgement is, that they do not like to appear ignorant of things, of which, nevertheless, they have neither experience nor knowledge.

Beyond obedience to superiors, which the Holy Spirit supports and inspires, we are also taught by the Holy Spirit to consult enlightened persons when the need arises, and to follow their opinion on certain matters. It is thus that St. Paul was referred to Ananias by the Lord, that he might learn from him what he ought to do. (Acts 9:6,12) Generally speaking, if we consult a spiritual person who is familiar with the ways of God, the various views and opinions presented will shed some light as to the right course of action under the circumstances, helping us to discern the will of God.

Now, if we do not experience the guidance of the Holy Spirit, perhaps we have not done what we can to dispose ourselves for it. If we are altogether exterior, scarcely ever entering into ourselves, and examining our conscience only very superficially, looking only to the outward man and the faults which are manifest in the eyes of the world, without seeking to discover their secret roots *(the capital sins)* and to become acquainted with our own predominant vices and sinful habits, without investigating the state of our soul and the movements of our heart, is it any wonder that we rarely, if ever, experience the guidance of the Holy Spirit, which is wholly interior. How can we know anything of it?—we do not even know our own interior sins which come from our own thoughts and desires. If we do not seek to remove the clutter and become more aware of the interior, how can we hear or receive the supernatural impressions, the inspired thoughts and desires, of the Holy Spirit which are quiet and gentle?

On the other hand, if we have done all that we can to dispose ourselves for the guidance of the Holy Spirit and still have little to no experience of it, we must be patient and persevere in the practice of prayer, virtue, and the sacraments, dying to ourselves and our sin, to our own ego and pride and self-will, until God gives us the grace of our Lord Jesus Christ and the gift of the Holy Spirit more fully. "Humble yourselves, therefore, under the mighty hand of God, that He may lift you up in due time *(in the time of visitation)*." (1 Peter 5:6) Also, we would do well, when providence provides, to lay bare our soul to another Christian, a spiritual and interior person, who can enlighten us about the things of God and the way to heaven, which is to say, the Way of Christ. A soul which acts thus, can hardly fail to receive, sooner or later, the guidance of the Holy Spirit, either directly or through another who is led by the Spirit of God.

The Goal of the Spiritual Life and the Guidance of the Holy Spirit:

The two parts of the spiritual life are the cleansing of the heart and the guidance of the Holy Spirit. These are the two poles of all true spirituality.

The whole essence of the spiritual life and of perfection consists in observing the ways and movements of the Spirit of God in our soul, and in strengthening our will and ability to follow them—as we die to our old way of life and sin and are filled with the New Man, Christ Jesus—employing for this purpose all the exercises of prayer, spiritual reading, the sacraments, the practice of virtue and of good works.

The goal to which we ought to aspire through the purification of the heart and faithful correspondence with the operations of the Holy Spirit, is to live no longer in ourselves, but in Jesus Christ, and to be so possessed and governed by His Spirit that He alone shall direct all our powers and faculties, both interior and exterior, while we, on our part, make a complete surrender of ourselves to Him, now that our rebellious inclinations have been subjugated to the power of His grace, and we have experienced the embrace of God in perfect peace—the divine union of our soul with Christ the Risen Lord in "divided tongues *(flames)* of fire" to the glory of God the Father. (Acts 2:3)

Devotion to Our Lord

(Spiritual Maxims)

*The remembrance of
the most holy Passion of Jesus Christ
(especially, when we suffer)
is the door through which the soul enters
into intimate union with God,
interior recollection and most sublime
contemplation.*
—St. Paul of the Cross

Christ is the center, not only of our religion, but of our whole spiritual life. By whatever path the soul may be led, whether in a more active life or a more contemplative life, Jesus Christ is the one guide and pattern, the chief subject of its meditation and contemplation, the object of its affection, the goal of its course. He is its

Physician, Shepherd, and King; He is its food and delight. And there is no other Name under heaven given to men, whereby they may be saved, or come to perfection. (Acts 4:12)

Therefore, it is both absurd and irreverent to imagine that there can be any prayer from which the humanity of Our Lord may or ought to be willfully excluded, as an object not sufficiently sublime or spiritual. Such an idea can be nothing but an illusion of the devil. Contemplate the perfections of God, if you are drawn to do so; lose yourself, if you will, in the Divine Essence; nothing is more legitimate or praiseworthy, provided grace gives you wings for the flight and humility is the companion of that sublime contemplation. But never fancy that it is a lower course to look and gaze upon the Savior, whenever He presents Himself to your mind. Such an error is the effect of a false spirituality and of a refined pride, and whether we are aware of it or not leads directly to disorders of the flesh, by which intellectual pride is almost invariably punished.

Know, then, that as long as the soul has free use of its faculties, whether in meditation, affective prayer, or the prayer of simple regard, it is primarily to Our Lord that we must turn. Pure contemplation, in which the faculties of intellect and free will are taken up into the presence of God with purely spiritual realities or truths, is too high for weak minds like ours, encumbered with a weight of flesh, and subjected in many ways to material things.

Furthermore, to seek God merely through general concepts and intellectual speculation, no matter how refined or subtle, is to end up disappointed and discouraged. This kind of "contemplation" or meditation is too bare and dry for the heart, which finds no nourishment therein. The abstract consideration of infinite perfection contains nothing to stimulate us to virtue, or sustain and encourage us when low. If pursued apart from God's will, it can leave the soul dry, cold, full of self-esteem, having disdain for others, distaste and contempt for vocal prayer (which in our weakness we need), and for the common practices of devotion, charity and humility, and indifferent to the sacraments, even the Most Blessed Sacrament.

So, we turn to Our Lord Jesus Christ, who is "the Way, the Truth, and the Life," for our prayer life, our spiritual life, our whole life. (John 14:6)

If, however, the powers of the soul are captivated by the presence of God in prayer, then it is possible that we may not be able to think of Our Lord in any particular way, or of any other subject for that matter. Notice that it is not the soul that brings this about, but God who withdraws the soul from the consideration of distinct or particular objects into the general and loving awareness of His presence in peace and solitude. Outside of these blessed times of pure and simple contemplation, the soul will continue to seek the face of Christ in active ways. It thirsts to be joined to Him in Holy Communion. It spends itself in holy aspirations *(short prayers)*. It seeks to be joined to Him in His mysteries, and adopts certain practices for that purpose, including the corporal and spiritual works of mercy. It seeks Him in spiritual reading, visits Him in His holy House *(the Church or chapel)*, and has recourse to Him in temptation — "dash your evil thoughts against Christ (Crucified) immediately." (St. Benedict) There is no Christian soul, really and truly interior, who does not strive to live in Him and by Him and for Him, and to have for Him a deep and continuous love.

How could it be otherwise? God the Father gave us His Son for this very purpose. He became man in order to unite us with Himself, by the power of the Holy Spirit. Sin had separated us so far from the Father; Christ came to repair that chasm— "No one comes to the Father, but by Me." (John 14:6) No one dwells in the Father, but by Him. To forget the sacred humanity of Our Lord would be to sever our sole link to the grace and friendship of the Holy Trinity.

St. Paul was not only an interior man, but a true contemplative in the mystical state, held "bound by the Holy Spirit," Who in a sovereign but free manner was the guide of all his thoughts, his feelings, his words, and of all he wrote; indeed, of the whole course of his apostolic work. (Acts 20:22) Can anyone doubt that he was a mystic to an extraordinary degree, in view of what he tells us of the greatness of his revelations, the humiliating temptations to which he was subject in order to keep him humble, and of the gifts of the Holy Spirit which he possessed in such plenitude? Yet his epistles are full of Christ; he speaks of nothing else, and with what transports of gratitude and love! The mere mention of the Holy Name is enough to send him into such raptures that his words cannot contain his thoughts, and pile up their images in the liveliest disorder in their endeavor to express the sublimity of his supernatural enthusiasm. Again and again, he urges the faithful to study Christ, to imitate Christ, to "put on" Christ, to do all and suffer all in the name of Christ. (Rom. 13:14)

St. Paul the Apostle invites the faithful to be followers of him as he is of Christ. (1 Cor. 11:1) He fills up in his own flesh what is still lacking in the sufferings of Christ for the sake of His Body, which is the Church. (Col. 1:24) That is, by his labors and sufferings he gains graces for the whole Church from the merits of Christ's Passion. Indeed, he even bears on his body "the marks of the Lord Jesus" as a sign of his sacrificial love for Christ and His Church. (Gal. 6:17) He spares himself in nothing until he can say, "I have been crucified with Christ; it is no longer I who live, but Christ who lives in me." (Gal. 2:20)

And what shall we say of St. John, the beloved disciple who, as the eagle dares to gaze with open eyes upon the sun, contemplated the eternal generation of the

Word in the Father? Not only literally, as at the Last Supper, but continuously throughout his life, he rested upon the heart of the Savior. And who ever reached a higher state of contemplation, or led a more interior life? And what is his Gospel but the most sublime and touching exposition, in the beauty of its depth and simplicity, of Jesus in His divine nature, and of all that He wants to be to us, and wants us to be to Him, as well as, of the most intimate desires of His Sacred Heart for the glory of the Father and the salvation of men? What are St. John's epistles but a tender exhortation for all people to love Christ, and to love one another even as He has loved us? What is the Apocalypse but a prophetic description of Christ, here below in His Church, and hereafter in the elect, washed and purified in His blood? St. John the Apostle was drawing near the end of his life and was consummated in the most perfect love of God and mystical union with Christ, when he received this divine vision and revelation from the Holy Spirit. In view of this, dare we say that there is a state of prayer so high that the Sacred Humanity has no place in it? Clearly not, unless we have lost our Way.

Among the saints, men and women, ancient and modern, were assuredly a great number of contemplatives who were highly advanced in the mystical life. Are there any to whom Christ and His mysteries were not the center and foundation of their prayer? Are there any who, in their writings, have not urgently proclaimed Our Lord as the unique Way that leads to perfection? There are none; there never have been, and there never will be.

You, then, who aspire to the interior life, that is to a life of genuine devotion *(love of God)*, enter, as the author of the *Imitation* counsels, into the hidden life of Jesus. Study to know Him well, to make His most intimate thoughts and attitude your thoughts and attitude, His desires your desires, His life your life. Let this knowledge of His life and virtues be the constant subject of your prayers, your spiritual reading and meditation, your life and action. Refer everything to the life of Christ as to its center and term. You will never exhaust it—you will not even fathom its depths. All of the saints discovered new treasures in the measure in which they advanced; they knew that "all the treasures of wisdom and knowledge" are hidden in

Christ. (Col 2:3) Indeed, they strove "to know the love of Christ which surpasses knowledge," and to be "filled with all the fullness of God." (Eph. 3:19)

For it is not enough to study Christ—we must stir our hearts to love Him, because the love of God and "the love of God made man" are one and the same thing. Let this love of Christ Our Lord be the food that feeds your soul, let it be the object of all your spiritual exercises, that you may grow in charity from day to day. "If any man love not our Lord Jesus Christ, let him be anathema; The Lord has come." (1 Cor. 16:22) To love Him in a half-hearted manner is to be but a weak or lukewarm Christian who will grow very little or not at all in the spiritual life, if they do not lose it altogether, because their heart is not in it to the full *(their intention to do the best they can is not 100%)*. The true Christian longs and strives to love the Lord Jesus more and more, knowing that He can never be loved as He deserves to be loved, or in the measure of His love for us.

But to love Him without imitating Him would be vain and fruitless. Therefore, be imitators of Christ. He is our model, perfect in every detail—a model for all states and for all conditions. To all people, in every conceivable circumstance, Christ in His mysteries *(the events of His life)*, in His virtues and in His doctrine, gives us the examples and lessons He proposes for our imitation. His teaching furnishes us with the most powerful motives for loving God and our neighbor, while His grace and the sacraments provide us with the most efficacious means.

But above all, meditate on His Passion; cling to His Passion, especially in your own temptations and trials, your own pain and suffering of whatever kind. Reproduce in your own life those virtues of which His Passion presents the most living picture *(for example—acceptance, humility, patience and perseverance, charity, forgiveness, mortification and fortitude, chastity, purity and abandonment to Divine Providence).* Seek in your prayers to draw love from His salutary wounds, above all from His pierced Heart. *("Into Your Sacred Heart, Jesus Christ Crucified, I abandon myself, now and forever, through the Immaculate Heart of Mary.")* Remember that His sacred Passion is the foundation of the whole of our faith—that He came on earth to die upon the Cross; that it was by this sacrifice He made satisfaction to the Father and expiation for our sins, thus opening up heaven to us and meriting, superabundantly, all of the graces that will bring us there. Remember that the sublime sacrifice of our altars—the offering of the Holy Sacrifice of the Mass—which is the central act of our faith, is but the memorial, the renewal and extension of the sacrifice of Calvary. And it was Our Lord Himself who said—"Do this in memory of Me." (Luke 22:19)

The crucifix is, and always will be, the dearest book of devout Christians who are Catholic. It speaks to the senses, to the mind and to the heart. No other language is so eloquent or so touching. It is within the understanding of the most simple and uneducated, yet is, at the same time, above the comprehension of the greatest intellect and the highest learning. It says all, teaches all, answers all. It calls forth and confirms the greatest efforts, consoles and sustains in times of the most bitter sorrow, and changes the very bitterness into sweetness.

The crucifix invites converted sinners to do penance, causing them to realize all the malice and enormity of their crimes *(against God's law)*—their sins and vices. It reproaches them with as much gentleness as force; offers them the remedy, assures them of pardon, and prompts in their hearts feelings of contrition as loving as they are sincere. It encourages the just who have been so mercifully forgiven to live a life of virtue for the Crucified One who loved them unto death. It persuades them to renounce and fight their passions, rendering them deaf to the cries of self-love, which dreads poverty, suffering and the afflictions that mortify the mind and body. Above all, it humiliates and destroys human pride, the source of all vice and sin.

The crucifix draws us to a state of recollection and prayer, to the interior life. It speaks to us of gentleness, patience, pardon for injuries done to us, love for our enemies, charity towards fellow Christians, even to the offering of our lives for them. It moves us to love God by revealing the extent of His love for all mankind, and how truly He deserves to be loved in return. It impels us to submission and the perfect conformity of our will to the divine will, whatever the cost, and to confidence and abandonment in times of the greatest desolation. In a word, it guides us to the practice of virtue and the avoidance of vice, in a way so gentle and persuasive that it is impossible for the Christian soul to refuse.

Devout soul, do you desire to attain to union with God, to receive the precious gift of His continual presence which makes all labor light? Then spend some time every day before the crucifix. Take no other subject for your meditation. Gaze at it, hold it in your hands, pray to Jesus hanging on the Cross, and ask Him to be your Teacher and Leader, your Guide and Director. *("Lord Jesus Christ, please teach me and lead me, guide me and direct me in the Way of Your will.")* Then, let go of your mind in His presence and let it be silent; let your heart alone speak. Hold onto His Sacred wounds and pierced side and abide in His loving presence. At times, your soul will be moved, and torrents of grace will flow into it, and with joy you will draw water out of the wells of salvation. (Isaiah 12:3) You will run in the way of His commandments, when He enlarges your heart and understanding, for the Cross contains all. (Psalms 119:32)

Say not, O Christian soul, that the sight *(or thought)* of the crucifix does no good for you, that it just leaves you cold and empty with nothing to say. If you cannot speak, you can listen. You can do some spiritual reading, along with prayers and affections. But then, stay silently and humbly at your Savior's feet, there with Mary, His Blessed Mother. If you persevere in prayer, the Lord will not fail to instruct, nourish, and fortify you. And if you feel nothing of this at the time, you will still perceive it in your conduct, and in the gradual change in your disposition, which will become more Christian. We are impatient, and our senses cry out to be satisfied, and, for this reason, we abandon the most profitable practices just because they do not succeed immediately. Persevere, I say. You have greatly abused the love of Jesus, by wasting His graces on self-satisfaction, let Him test your love a little. He will crown your perseverance with success, and give you the gift of infused prayer *(contemplation)* as a reward and blessing.

Our Lord's Passion has always been the particular devotion of those saints who have been renowned for their hidden life. Such were St. Bernard, St. Francis of Assisi, St. Bridget of Sweden, St. John of the Cross, St. Catherine of Siena, St. Paul of the Cross, St. Teresa of Avila and many others. Yet, if some of these great mystics tell us in their writings that there are states of soul in which one loses sight of Our Lord, they will always add that these spiritual experiences are the expression of stages in Christ's own life, and that it is He Who impresses on the soul His own dispositions as He grew from childhood to His death, and then, in His Resurrection and Ascension. Step by step Jesus leads us to pass through these various stages, commencing with sensible joys, and passing to exterior and inner sufferings both of body and soul; humiliations, contradictions, calumnies and persecutions on the part of others; temptations on the part of the devil, and trials and interior aridity on the part of God *(—until coming, through Christ our Lord, to a spiritual resurrection, or later and in parallel fashion, to a spiritual ascension and transformation in Christ Jesus our Lord).*

During these trials, we do not always see that it is Our Lord Who is crucifying us in order to free us from ourselves so that we can be united to Him. When, in His goodness and wisdom, Jesus hides Himself from us, we suffer more, it is true, but with greater merit, because we need more faith and hope and charity, which He supplies, and with greater security because we are less likely to go off into spiritual pride or vainglory which would contradict His work of destroying the "old man" and building the "New"—"until Christ be formed in you." (Gal. 4:19)

Thus, during these purifications, we are never more truly and intimately united with Our Lord than when there seems to be a thick veil between Him and our soul, which we would like to lift but cannot. At these times of mystical darkness, even though we are unable to concentrate on His life and mysteries in the particular, we are united to Christ in the interior of our heart and soul by good will and desire. We cannot see Him, but we love Him, because His love is somewhere deep inside of us, and He is deep inside of us, though hidden in the cloud of contemplation. This is not Quietism because the soul is actively engaged in knowing and loving the Lord in a general way, "in spirit and in truth," our heart and mind and soul being then absorbed in the Divine presence. (John 4:24)

When our faculties are not being held in suspension by the Divine presence, or, more generally, not resting in the "cloud of unknowing" or infused contemplation, let us again look to Our Lord in His mysteries, especially, as found in the Sacred Liturgy, while leaving it up to the Holy Spirit to guide, direct, and move us, applying ourselves to either meditation or contemplation in the manner and to the degree that God wills.

Made in the USA
Columbia, SC
26 August 2019